Walking In Their Shoes

Communicating with loved ones who have Alzheimer's disease

MICHAEL KRAUTHAMER

authorHOUSE®

AuthorHouse™
1663 Liberty Drive
Bloomington, IN 47403
www.authorhouse.com
Phone: 1-800-839-8640

First published by AuthorHouse 9/24/2010

ISBN: 978-1-4520-5862-7 (e)
ISBN: 978-1-4520-5860-3 (sc)
ISBN: 978-1-4520-5861-0 (hc)

Library of Congress Control Number: 2010912392

Printed in the United States of America

"And what is as important as knowledge, asked the mind? Caring and seeing with the heart, answered the soul."

-Anonymous

*Dedicated with
love and appreciation to:*

*My parents who taught me to strive for my
dreams without compromising my ethics,
morals, and values. Even today, they continue
to inspire and teach by their example.*

Contents

Introduction

Negative behaviors associated with Alzheimer's disease can develop for many different reasons, such as pain, confusion, isolation, anxiety, anger, and distorted sense of time. Because "behaviors" are a form of communication, understanding what causes them is important in understanding and resolving them.

If you are reading this book, chances are you know someone diagnosed with Alzheimer's disease. This book will demonstrate how to communicate with your loved one better and assist you in understanding how some behaviors originate. After ten years of working with persons diagnosed with Alzheimer's disease, I have composed a collection of true stories about the many positive experiences I have participated in and observed.

Many people question whether persons diagnosed with moderate-to-severe Alzheimer's disease can understand or communicate. Some question whether their family member or friend knows them. I believe that many *can* communicate and many know their family or friends, regardless of whether they can verbally communicate. Although their form of communication may change, they still have the ability to communicate, just in a different manner. I learned that successful communication was achieved through validating the feelings, or reality that the person *believed* they lived in.

Utilizing the sociological model of healthcare (person-centered care) and "Validation Therapy," which is a form of therapy discovered and developed by Naomi Feil, I learned quickly that meaningful communication could be achieved with persons who were previously believed to be non-communicative. In addition, "behaviors" could be easily redirected, diminished, or eliminated once I understood what caused the behavior. Time after time, these techniques were very effective. The same techniques were used in three different socio-economic settings, frequently with the same positive results. Although these techniques were not effective every time, people were receptive most of the time. And when they were receptive, the techniques facilitated communication, improved communication, assisted in understanding the meaning of a behavior, or how to redirect or resolve it.

Forward

As the saying goes, "Take a walk in my shoes and you will better understand me." Although you can never really walk in someone else's shoes, you can try to understand where their shoes have walked. In this book, I invite you to take a journey with me and persons diagnosed with moderate-to-severe Alzheimer's disease. The journey will cover many miles and spans of time. As we travel the miles, the landscape will change, as does the reality for the people we will be walking with. At the conclusion of our journey, you will better understand the rationale of the residents whom we are fortunate to walk with. You will better understand what many health professionals name "behaviors" and also how easy it is to diminish, redirect, or eliminate these behaviors.

At the time this book was published, an estimated 5.3 million Americans were diagnosed with Alzheimer's disease. This tragic disease continues to grow as the baby boomers come of age. It is estimated between the years 2010 and 2030, 17 million people will become at high risk to develop Alzheimer's disease.[1] It is important that you see the faces and realities of these people, not just the numbers. My book is designed to assist you in exploring the reality, and face, of Alzheimer's

---

1 "2010 Alzheimer's Disease Facts And Figures," Prevalence, pages 10,11,12: Alzheimer's Association.

disease by inviting you on a short journey into the world of Alzheimer's disease.

Almost immediately upon employment, I realized how easy and often meaningful communication could be achieved with people who were believed to be non-commutative, using two simple techniques that I had learned while attending Indiana University.

When someone truly believes they are living in a different reality, I have learned that if I can calm someone, help them feel less lonely or confused, stop a behavior, or make someone happy, I will use a therapeutic fib. When needed, I carefully use this technique, which others may call lying. You will also read about the positive experiences with Validation Therapy. Simply stated, validation means to "validate" the belief, feelings, or reality of another person. As you will witness, practiced in the right manner with empathy, understanding, love, and patience, using therapeutic fibbing and validation can result in a successful resolution to a negative situation.

This book is written for *all* health care providers, whether personal or professional, and with the utmost respect and empathy for the individuals and their families who allowed me to become a part of their world and the *individual's reality*. While working in long-term healthcare, I recognized the need for an easy-to-read handbook that tells real stories from my experiences. This book illustrates how easy it is to successfully use these techniques. You will see that communication is possible and comes in all shapes, sizes, and realities. When used properly, this form of communication is a powerful tool that can decrease or eliminate behaviors.

One of the golden rules of communicating with persons diagnosed with Alzheimer's disease is **NEVER ARGUE**. Arguing only creates a dysfunctional environment that can cause depression, loneliness, confusion, behaviors, and detachment. Therefore, remember to never argue or contradict. It is extremely important that discretion is used with these valuable techniques. Validating someone's feelings or beliefs can become detrimental when the person truly believes that something bad is happening. In this instance, while accepting their reality, choose carefully what you validate and always ensure them they are safe.

It is important to gather as much information as possible from the patient while you are validating their reality. Many times, people are reliving their past experiences, therefore it is of great importance to obtain a personal social history from a relative or friend. You will better understand what the person is experiencing and the history will assist you in validating their reality. Sometimes it is difficult to obtain a social history. If that's the case, it is always **important to listen** and try to piece together the true feelings or experiences you will validate. The more information you receive, the easier the techniques become. You may be validating the same feelings or thoughts on a regular basis, but experience teaches that nothing is ever written in stone, so it is always important to use discretion on what feelings or beliefs you are validating.

The Journey Begins

A Rural Farming Community

After graduation, I was fortunate to be offered employment in a dual position as Social Service Director and Activity Director working with persons diagnosed with Alzheimer's disease. My first employer, was in a wealthy farming community an hour and a half from my home. The facility owners had researched architectural designs specific to the needs of Alzheimer's disease and built a state of the art lock-down unit. This architectural model correlated with the sociological model of healthcare (person-centered care) that I had studied in college. My first workday was beautiful and sunny and made the "first day jitters" diminish as I drove through the colorful landscape of clouds and hills.

After winding through the unfamiliar, wooded hills, I finally arrived. As I began walking to the door with my laptop computer, I noticed a sign in bold letters: "TO ENTER, PRESS 4321." The security code was designed to keep the residents with moderate and severe cognitive impairment safely inside. When a person reaches this point of impairment, it is important that caregivers provide a safe environment that promotes their physical and psychosocial well-being. Just as important is to maintain their dignity and respect. As I pushed the buttons on the security pad and heard the heavy doors unlock, I began to comprehend the gravity of my new vocation and the uncertain challenges of my journey.

I walked through the doors only to find another set of doors with the same sign. The double doors were designed as a barrier in case one of the residents exited the first set of doors. They were approximately 8 feet apart. As an added precaution, an alarm sounded when any door was opened for a predetermined amount of time. If a resident somehow made it through the first set of doors, it was highly unlikely that they would make it through the second, due to the inability to comprehend, or even see the words that clearly explained how to enter and exit.

Opening the second door revealed a long, narrow hallway decorated in a warm home-like style with richly colored wallpaper, carpeting, and nicely framed paintings. People were walking, standing, and sitting in wheelchairs. At first appearance, the hallway was like any other with people mingling and doing their daily business. Walking down the hallway with a smile, I greeted every resident with a "Good Morning." As I continued walking, I realized that I had entered a world where my reality and the reality of others were in direct contradiction. More importantly, the only reality that mattered was in the minds of these people because that was *their true reality*.

Several of the residents caught my attention as I wondered about their life history and experiences. Harold, a frail, gray-haired, 94-year-old, was sitting in his wheelchair glaring at me as I proceeded down the hallway and into my new office. Due to his frail condition, Harold was at risk for falling; therefore, he had a pull tab alarm connected to him and his wheelchair to notify staff if he tried to stand.

One day, sitting in my office, I heard a loud commotion in the hallway as a high-pitched alarm blared. I immediately ran to the location where I found Harold and a staff member in a heated argument screaming over the blaring alarm. The staff member was yelling, "Sit down, Harold!" as Harold was yelling, "I don't have to!" It was apparent that neither person was going to win the argument or stop yelling. Finally, a nurse arrived and intervened. In a calm voice, she changed the subject and persuaded Harold to sit down. At this point, it is important to discuss a major rule of communication. Never argue with a person who is diagnosed with Alzheimer's disease. In addition to creating hostility, it can invoke many more emotions, from sadness and loneliness to confusion. Even if they cannot understand your words, they do understand your nonverbal communication and tone of voice. Sometimes they even mirror it. Therefore, it is important that as friends, family or healthcare providers, we monitor our own behavior such as mood, tone of voice, attitude, and mannerisms, especially with those who have lost verbal communication skills or speak in a nonsensical manner. Sometimes they no longer comprehend the spoken word, so it is imperative to enhance communication through nonverbal means.

After reading Harold's psychosocial history and learning more about him, I gained much insight into his previous life. He had been a very successful farmer, and among other animals and crops, he had raised hogs. Although Harold had lived in the facility for more than one year, it was quite clear that he still believed that he was living on his 950-acre farm. In his mind, he was not living in present time but had a very *different reality*, in which he was still living on his farm. Nevertheless, whatever Harold believed was his truth, *his reality*, and nothing anyone said could change his mind.

With the information obtained from his social history and a better understanding, I had a meeting with the staff and suggested that when Harold stood up, instead of yelling at him to sit down, they should walk over and ask in a calm voice, "Harold, where are you going?" After my request, it seemed like an eternity before I would hear his alarm sound again. When it did, I looked up and sure enough, he was trying to stand. He was in such a fragile physical state that he couldn't stand, let alone walk. My concern was that he would fall and hurt himself. As the alarm sounded, I ran to him in the hallway. In a calm voice, while making eye contact, I said, "Hey Harold, where ya goin'?" Harold's stone cold eyes glared into mine as he stated, "I am goin' to feed my hogs." Trying to think fast, I said "Harold, I just fed your hogs." With some confusion showing on his face, he said, "You did?" "Yes, Harold, I just walked back in. It sure is cold out there." With that statement, he slowly sat back down as the alarm stopped sounding. Wow, my first experience with validation therapy and it worked! Harold was happy that his hogs had been fed and I was happy that he was sitting down. I couldn't wait until I could try using validation again.

After much observation and many trips to his wheelchair, I realized that there were several reasons why Harold wanted to stand up. As long as I approached him in a calm manner and said, "Where ya goin?" he would always tell me where he believed he needed to go. Whether he needed to feed his livestock, pick up his tractor or go to the bathroom, his needs were always met. Acting quickly was important, because if the staff didn't reach Harold when he had to urinate, believing he was "living on the farm," he would urinate wherever he happened to be.

One day, while walking down the hallway, I heard someone yelling and cursing inside his room. As I knocked on the door and entered, Harold was partially sitting up in his bed, leaning on his elbows and yelling, "Who told those sons of bitches they could drive on my property?" Harold was hearing and seeing the traffic on the street outside the window. His question caught me off guard and I blurted out, "Well, Harold, they put a road on your property." Harold snapped back, "I didn't give anybody permission to put a road on my property! Who did it? They must have paid me good money to put a road there." At that point, the only words that came to my mind were that it was the government and they had a lot of money and needed to put the road there so people could make it to the other side. With that explanation, Harold calmed down and resumed his nap. So, validating that Harold owned the property and using a therapeutic fib stating that he was paid good money for the road was successful. Harold pretty much kept to himself except when he needed something, and didn't associate with the staff or residents except when approached. But he did enjoy it when Cindy and Beulah baked, assisted by the staff, which was usually me.

Cindy and Beulah

Cindy and Beulah were roommates but that was their only common tie. In the past, both women had worked, raised families, and had many similarities, but they could no longer verbally communicate so they lived in separate worlds. Both Cindy and Beulah had very supportive families who provided a great deal of social history. But when Cindy spoke, she was usually nonsensical, and Beulah never verbally communicated.

Cindy had beautiful gray hair that she had set every week by the facility hairstylist. She dressed well and had an insatiable curiosity. She enjoyed baking, spending time with grandchildren, and walking up and down the hallway. In the beginning, I believed that Cindy was a "classic wanderer." A classic wanderer is someone who walks aimlessly without destination or concern for safety. They continually walk for no known reason. But after interviewing her family, I discovered she had been in an automobile accident many years ago. Doctors had told her she would never walk again. But Cindy defied the odds and recovered. From then on, she walked everywhere. She walked to work, to purchase groceries, and thoroughly enjoyed walking. During her walks, if I would ask her where she was going, she would either ignore me and keep walking, or reply in a nonsensical manner. I tried to pick out words she repeated often but usually I could not make sense of the few words she spoke.

Sometimes we would walk together until we arrived at her destination, which was one end of the hallway or the other. She never stopped or slowed down while walking so I walked alongside her as we talked. Cindy didn't speak often, but sometimes when I asked her a question, she would reply. She usually sat alone wherever she decided except on her frequent walks that usually took place during the most inopportune times, such as meal times.

She always appeared to be looking for something to do, or somewhere to go. Because she really didn't verbally communicate, the nurse decided to place a life-like baby doll in a small crib in one of Cindy's usual destinations. Sometimes a person picks up the "baby" and sometimes not. The next time Cindy wandered to her usual destination she walked back holding the baby doll in her arms just like a newborn mother. From then on the "baby" was always with her. Taking care of this baby was Cindy's responsibility. Cindy had raised three girls and knew exactly what to do. She changed the baby, dressed the baby, fed the baby and most importantly, she loved the baby. Although it became difficult getting the baby from her so the staff could clean the dried foods from the mouth, or change soiled clothing, we could see the positive change in Cindy's life since she found this doll who she truly believed was a real baby. One day the nurse noticed that Cindy was not acting like her usual self. She appeared very upset and distraught while talking to the baby.

On this day, she was speaking in a nonsensical manner but was clearly concerned about the baby's health. Cindy was saying in a distressed, frightened tone that sometimes babies can get sick and die, and other horrible comments. At this point, the nurse and I decided we must go into Cindy's reality to try and resolve her negative, frightened state of mind. We had never witnessed Cindy this upset, and sat down with her and the doll. The nurse had a thermometer, tongue depressor, and stethoscope. The nurse took the doll and explained to Cindy that she was a nurse and was going to give the baby a physical exam. As the nurse checked the baby's heart, temperature, mouth, eyes, and ears, she clearly explained each procedure to Cindy. After she was finished, she assured her that her baby was in good health. Cindy smiled as we returned the baby to her arms.

Later that day when talking to her family, we learned that several years before, Cindy had been taking care of her grandchildren and gave one of them the wrong dosage of medicine. The child was rushed to the hospital. Once again, this situation illustrates the need to know social histories because you can better understand the reality the person is living in. This knowledge becomes very important when validating someone's feelings or using a therapeutic fib.

Beulah, whose hands had a tremor, never verbalized and

rarely made eye contact but would sit with the group when we were doing activities. Usually, she wouldn't participate but when given a magazine or book, she would stare into the pages, turning them as if she were reading. Every day, I would tell the residents that I was going to the post office and if anyone wanted to write a letter, I would mail it. Of all the people, I never would have guessed that Beulah would have accepted my offer. When I talked to Beulah, I didn't know if she even heard or understood what I was saying, but every time I would say I was going to the post office, Beulah would write a letter. I would give her paper and a pen and she usually spent around an hour composing her letter. When she was finished, I would take it and tell her I would mail it. All Beulah's letters were dated in the 1950s. Although she wrote each sentence twice and her writing was very shaky, her family was surprised that she could even write and amazed that her writings were historically accurate. The family was given a sense of hope that somewhere inside, their mother still remained. Once we knew that she was living in the 1950s, we could discuss current events *in her reality*. In addition, we found music from the era in which she lived. Beulah enjoyed this music immensely. While Cindy and I baked, Beulah would sit as if no one were there and read, while Harold and Ralph sat and waited for us to finish so that they could eat.

Ralph

One day, a family visited and discussed with me the possibility of moving their father into the facility. Ralph's wife had died two years ago and he had lived alone since her death. He was a farmer still living on his farm in a small rural community. His neighbors, who lived about a mile from his home, were trying to watch out for their neighbor but it was difficult. They noticed Ralph was not getting more and more chores done around his farm, and many times in the evening they would drive by and there were never lights on in his home. Ralph had lived his whole adult life on this farm, raising a family and running his business. In fact, he was still trying to take care of the farm, but according to his neighbors, he was becoming more and more confused and forgetful. He was still driving until one recent day when he became lost and didn't know where he was or how to get home. Ralph stopped at the local hardware store to ask for directions. Luckily, an employee at the hardware store knew him, drove him home, and contacted the family.

The family, who lived over an hour away, became concerned for his well-being and decided to look for a safe place for him to live that was close by them. The family provided a great deal of information concerning Ralph's social history. I cannot emphasize enough the importance of obtaining a social history for all residents entering a healthcare facility. Also, it is vital to confirm the history if you are unsure of its accuracy.

Because Ralph was in the beginning stages of Alzheimer's disease and could not move in with his family, we discussed the importance of preserving his dignity and respect during the move. We used "therapeutic fibbing" so Ralph would believe that he was making his own decision and was part of the moving process. After all, he was an adult who had raised a family and successfully worked his farm. He was just becoming confused.

More importantly, he understood his situation and the need for assistance. Nevertheless, the decision to move from his farm was a difficult proposition, even if he would be closer to his family. So there was no way that we would treat him like a child and make his decisions for him, or allow him to believe we had. We hoped he would believe he had made the decision. At this point, we scheduled an interview for Ralph to tour the facility.

Ralph and his family arrived on a sunny day. I gave them a tour and we purposely avoided any words sounding like "healthcare." We toured the outside garden, dining room, and if he chose to continue, we would show him the room he would be "renting." Ralph knew that he had some memory problems but couldn't understand why he had to move from his farm that he had owned for more than 50 years. He agreed with his family that it would be nice to live closer to them and he wouldn't have to worry about cooking. But he just couldn't understand why he would have to leave his farm. What would happen to it? He didn't know if it was necessary to leave his home or if he would like his room after he moved. Of course, the family and I took his concerns seriously. To succeed, we needed to ensure that Ralph was at ease with *his* decision and his new environment even though I knew that the family had already made the decision.

After several weeks, Ralph, a soft-spoken man who looked younger than his 84 years, returned to the facility with his family, suitcase in hand. He had decided to stay for a few days just to see how he would like his room and new environment. From Ralph's social history, I knew that he preferred keeping to himself, loved to watch college basketball, and enjoyed working on the farm and building birdhouses. I purchased some birdhouse kits and researched his favorite basketball teams and game times so Ralph could participate in familiar activities that he enjoyed. On his first day, I asked if he would like to help me build a birdhouse. He politely declined. I explained that I had never built a birdhouse and I was sure he could teach me a lot. But Ralph continued to decline my offer for several weeks, still not understanding why he had to move from his farm and why he was now "locked in" a building. Ralph had not noticed when he toured the facility that there were two sets of alarmed doors at the entrance. He explained that he had always been able to go outdoors whenever he wanted and couldn't understand why he was locked in the building. Ralph was very high-functioning, so therapeutic fibbing was not always appropriate. I would not even make an attempt for fear that Ralph would catch me. Once again, each individual is diverse and unique in their needs and many times therapeutic fibbing and validation are not appropriate. Ralph and I spent many hours discussing his family and why he was moved to the facility. Every time we talked, we discussed the locked doors and I always agreed that it was unfair to him. Because Ralph enjoyed staying busy I thought he was the ideal candidate for some "therapeutic chores."

Therapeutic chores, or work, can be any activity. Many people prefer to stay busy. So, any activity that they are familiar with, such as dusting, laundry, sweeping the floor, paperwork, light yard work, etc., is appropriate. Therapeutic chores are a wonderful way to keep people physically active and their mind engaged. In addition, it provides them a sense of familiarity and also being helpful, or needed, which increases their psychosocial well-being. It also gives people a purpose in life. Knowing that Ralph wanted to stay busy and enjoyed helping others, I came up with an idea that might engage Ralph.

One sunny day, I asked Ralph if he could do me a favor. Looking puzzled, Ralph said, "Well, I don't know…depends on what it is." I explained to him that I didn't have enough time to rake the leaves in the garden and they were really piling up. The garden was enclosed with tall fences and security cameras so the staff could monitor outdoor activities. With a smile, Ralph said "Well, I have raked a lot of leaves in my life so I am sure I can help you." As soon as he agreed, his physician was called to ensure he was physically healthy enough to rake leaves. With the physician's consent, a therapeutic order was placed in his chart. The day that Ralph helped me rake leaves brought great joy not only to Ralph but to the staff. His demeanor instantly changed. He was so proud of his accomplishment and the staff was quick to remind him of what a wonderful job he had performed. In his face and demeanor, you could see the great sense of accomplishment he felt by being useful. From that day on, Ralph always checked to see if there were any leaves for him to rake, and a rake was always located outside by the garden door.

Ralph and I had built a great rapport and I could see this soft-spoken, confused ex-farmer becoming a little more comfortable with his surroundings. Due to his changing attitude, I decided to return to building a bird house just to see if he had changed his mind on helping. "Ralph," I said, "I bought these birdhouses but I can't figure out how to put them together. I would really appreciate it if you could help me try and figure it out." With a smile, Ralph said, "Well, I used to build birdhouses, so let's give it a shot."

When the time arrived, I laid out all the pieces of the birdhouse kit on the table with a hammer and some nails along with the instructions. I observed that Ralph did not notice that the kit pieces were numbered. We began picking up the wooden pieces to see if we could fit the pre-cut pieces together. Much to my dismay, I looked up to see Ralph looking confused while trying to hold two pieces that did not fit. They were both end pieces, one designed for the front and other for the back. Until then, I was not aware that Ralph could not distinguish the difference between the size and shape of the pieces even though he had built elaborate birdhouses for many years. Quickly, I picked up the correct piece and said, "Oh, here is another piece, do you think this will work?"

Working together, we spent around an hour as we both patiently figured out how to build the birdhouse. Once we had the pieces glued together, we needed to nail it together. I watched as Ralph tried to nail two, then three nails into the same hole. Calmly, I said, "Ralph, maybe we should put a nail over there." After the nail was hammered in and when Ralph was in the bathroom, I hurriedly nailed all the pieces to finish the project. When Ralph returned, I showed him the birdhouse and we both agreed it was finished except for painting. I learned valuable information about Ralph and never suggested any more projects such as birdhouses. I never wanted to place him in a situation where he might become confused. It is good to stimulate a person's cognition, but if you observe frustration or confusion, stop the activity immediately.

Although the birdhouse didn't work as well as I would have liked, I remembered that Ralph had a passion for basketball. But, he never turned on the television in his room. I remembered that his family had told me about his passion for college basketball and old westerns, so one day I asked if he was receiving good reception on his TV. He responded in his usual timid manner, but this time it seemed as though he were trying to hide something. He said he didn't really like to watch TV. So everyday I would slip something into our conversation about a TV or basketball game so I could observe his response. He was such a private person that I did not want him thinking I was prying into his business. But I did want to better understand why he wasn't doing an activity he had enjoyed his whole life. About a week later during our daily television discussion, Ralph explained to me that his television was broken and he hadn't been able to use it. I informed him I would look at his television and see if I could fix it.

When I arrived and turned on the TV, it worked great. "How did you get that to work?" said Ralph. I replied, "I pushed this button" while pointing to the ON/OFF button. Ralph explained to me that the TV was broken and hadn't been working for him, and I listened. When our discussion ended, I found his favorite channel and told him if he had any more trouble to let me or the staff know and we would fix it.

After I left his room, I wondered how this man who could hide his cognitive loss with small talk, lived alone in his home, paying his bills and performing daily tasks when he couldn't figure out how to turn on the television. Because Ralph was a man of few words except for the occasional joke that he often repeated, he was an expert in small talk and hiding his cognitive loss. Although a large diagram was made and placed on the wall, Ralph could never figure out how to turn the television on or off. Everyday, I would check and find the power cord pulled out of the outlet. After the first time I questioned him about the cord, I realized he just couldn't understand.

To ensure Ralph's dignity and respect, and provide for his enjoyment, I produced a college basketball schedule for Ralph and the staff. The basketball schedule, along with other television shows, was posted at the nurse's station. The staff would ensure that the television was turned on with the correct channel. After he fell asleep, they would go in and turn off the television. They always did so in a manner to protect the dignity and respect of this very private, yet proud man. Once the television situation was resolved, Ralph became more receptive. Although Ralph had adapted to his new environment, unbeknownst to me, my environment was on the verge of change. The road in my journey turned to a new direction when I accepted a position in the suburbs of a large city.

The Suburbs

The Suburbs

As the Activity Director, my new employment offered me the opportunity to implement the sociological model of healthcare in a 40-bed Alzheimer's unit. In the suburbs of this large city, I learned that validation and therapeutic fibbing worked in all socioeconomic backgrounds. My new position was in a facility with a reputation for accepting patients with "behaviors." Many of the patients[2] had been classified as people who were difficult, and many had negative behaviors that were uncontrollable. Most of the patients had moderate-to-severe cognitive impairment. And many of them were prescribed strong medication. Early on, I learned that the residents weren't having behaviors; instead they were living in a different time and place. They lived in their *own reality*...a reality that was very real to them. I believed many of the behaviors were created by the staff who didn't accept the residents' reality and wanted to force them into our

---

2 Patient and Resident are interchangeable. Usually, once a patient enters a long-term healthcare facility to live, the name usually changes to resident.

world. This was an impossible task that created the patients' behaviors.

Most days, a group of women sat by the alarmed doors in the large front sitting area. This area included two couches with end tables and two large chairs. The double doors had been painted to look like a bookcase to disguise the door and many residents didn't realize that the huge bookshelf with books and knick-knacks was really alarmed doors. These women, who all had their purses and were prepared to leave for different destinations, were always congregated in the sitting area and ready to leave as soon as someone opened the door. At the same time, they didn't realize it was a door until someone walked through. Some were expecting company, or waiting for the bus or their ride. To be successful in validating their feelings, I needed to learn their reality. With a smile, I would ask each lady, "Where are you going today?" Some would tell me that they were going home, waiting for someone, or getting ready to go to wherever they believed they were going. Their responses never changed. Most of the women didn't have frequent visitors and some of them had none at all. But, in their reality, they did have visitors, a home, places to go and people to see.

If I asked them their address, they would tell me an address that usually was an accurate address for someone who had been significant in their life, and sometimes they would tell me their previous address or an address from the past. It was uncanny to me how people could remember a previous address, but not be able to tell me their name. Many days, meal times were a difficult task because the women did not want to leave the sitting area for fear that they might miss their company, ride, or opportunity to leave. When meal time would roll around, it was important that these residents felt secure enough about leaving the sitting area to move to the dining room. I told the residents whatever I needed to say to convince them to eat. Sometimes, a lot of convincing was needed and other times, the task was easy.

Meals are provided at scheduled times in most healthcare facilities. About half an hour before meals, I would begin the task of talking to the women to see what their reality was. Once I obtained this information, I would begin validating their feelings and use therapeutic fibs so they would feel secure enough to leave and eat their meal. Sometimes after their meal, they would forget that they were waiting for their ride, or having company, and move on to other activities, and other times they would return to wait. Because of the importance of other activities such as exercise and personal care, making the women feel secure enough to leave the sitting area was extremely important, and each time I made sure to do it with patience and persistence.

Therefore, if someone was waiting for a ride, I might tell them that the person called to say they were having car trouble and wouldn't be able to give them a ride. Many times, questions ensued and I would continue to use therapeutic fibs until they felt secure enough to leave.

One day as I returned from lunch, a 92-year-old woman rushed up to me, crying, as she said, "Is my mother dead?" Of course, this question caught me off guard and I replied,

"I don't know. When did you last talk to her?" She explained that she had just talked to her, so I replied, "What was she doing?" The woman explained that her mother was getting ready to cook lunch and had been cleaning the house. After a discussion with her, I realized that a nurse had told her that her mother was dead. Of course, when you are 92, the chances are high that your mother may not be alive but the only fact that mattered was whether she believed she was. I assured her that her mother must still be alive if she just talked to her. With this statement, she left with a smile.

You must always be sincere when utilizing therapeutic fibbing and *with all* communication because the person may interpret a different message from your tone of voice or body language. Long after a person losses their ability to verbally communicate, they retain their ability to understand nonverbal communication.

Juanita and Mary

Juanita, a tall, stately, slender woman who walked with a cane and slight limp, had retired from nursing. This quiet yet dignified woman was diagnosed with Alzheimer's disease combined with audio/visual hallucinations. Some days, she believed that she still worked as a nurse and other days, she had forgotten. Often in Juanita's mind, her dog, Peppy, was by her side. Although Juanita was the only person who saw or heard Peppy, he was very real to her. He lived in *her reality*.

One day, while working in my office, I overheard loud voices at the nurse's station. Juanita, in an angry voice, yelled, "Peppy told me that you owe me $20.00 from that check I gave you!" Of course, no check had been written and no money was owed but I listened further. "I don't owe you any money and you didn't give me a check," the nurse shouted. "Yes, you do, Peppy was watching you and he doesn't lie. You do owe me another $20.00!" Juanita said. At this time, a shouting match ensued and I overheard the nurse tell another staff member to go and find another nurse to assist her in giving Juanita a

PRN shot (a PRN is a prescribed medication only to be given, if needed) for medical need, or in this case, a "behavior."

When I heard the nurse instruct the staff member, I jumped up from my desk, grabbed a legal pad and immediately ran out of my office to find the nurse and resident continuing their heated argument. Politely, in a calm tone I interrupted, "Miss Juanita, I heard that someone owes you some money and I am here to do an investigation. Can we sit over here so I can get some information?" Juanita looked at me with relief and said, "Yes, I would appreciate your help." As we set down, I said, "So I hear that you are owed some money." "Yes," she continued, "Peppy said that woman behind the desk didn't give me all my money and she still owes me $20." Of course, there was no Peppy, but she believed that he was sitting beside her and she could see him. So when she brought up Peppy, I decided that I would ask her what kind of dog Peppy was. "You know, I don't know very much about dogs. What kind of dog is Peppy?" She was happy to reply that Peppy was a male poodle and that her mother and father had bred poodles when she was growing up. She continued by telling me that she had always loved animals, but poodles were her favorite by far. At this point, Juanita had completely forgotten the argument over $20 when two nurses approached her with a syringe.

"Juanita, can you come in here so we can talk to you?" The nurses wanted her to go in the shower room so they could give her a powerful medication to reduce her "behavior." "What do you want to talk to me about?" asked Juanita. "You know. . .the money I owe you," replied the nurse. Juanita did not need a shot at any point. But, the nurses convinced her to go with them into the shower room. Without success, I strongly voiced my concerns to the nurses, trying to explain that the medication was not needed. The nurse proceeded with her plan. For the rest of the day, Juanita sat slumped over in a cloudy haze from the medication she had been given.

Although it is sometimes a necessity, I do not believe in medicating persons for being confused, and always believe we should try to resolve the situation through verbal and nonverbal communication. In addition, at least three attempts should be made before any medication is even considered. Residents have the right to be free from physical and chemical restraints unless they are a danger to themselves or others. In this case, the nurse, a healthcare professional, was antagonizing the resident to the point of great anger. This was unacceptable behavior by the nurse.

The need for validation is overwhelming when it comes to disruptive behaviors or when someone is upset. The whole point is to calm them down and allow them to remain in their reality, thereby giving them a sense of security. In this situation, the nurse created the behavior and could have resolved, instead of contributed to, the resident's anger. Simply by stating, "I am sorry I didn't give you all the money, I must have miscounted but I will give it to you as soon as I can," or with any other reasoning the situation could have been successfully resolved without the need for chemical intervention.

Maintaining a calm demeanor is always one key to success

when communicating to someone who is confused and agitated. When proper techniques are used, there is no longer a need for powerful medication. In fact, this conflict affected not only Juanita but the other residents. One woman in particular who was standing next to Juanita stared as the situation unfolded. Mary, who appeared distraught, had witnessed the argument. You could see in her face that she knew something bad was going on between the nurse and Juanita. Her body language revealed that she was becoming more and more anxious.

Mary was a quiet woman who always appeared distraught, confused, nervous, or depressed. Her mood was easily displayed through her body language.

Many days, she sat or walked alone, looking like a lost soul with nothing to do. She always appeared isolated, living in a world of her own. She didn't speak often, but when she did, her speech was nonsensical. It was a difficult task to get Mary involved in activities. Because her communication was more nonverbal than verbal, I never knew if Mary understood my verbal message so I would always "cue" her with my body language and hand gestures.

Some days, I observed Mary talking to her roommate in the dining room. Her roommate also spoke nonsensically. I was always perplexed by how these women could carry on conversations that made no sense to anyone but them. Nevertheless, they conversed and appeared to communicate and that was all that mattered. Due to Mary's inability to effectively verbally communicate, I was concerned for her psychosocial well-being. Most days, she wondered around as if she were looking for something to do. Sometimes she could be encouraged to become involved in exercise or balloon toss, but she never quite understood how to participate. When she did attend, it was apparent that she was nervous and not certain how to act. She appeared as if she were trying to fit in with the group but somehow just didn't. This sad, nervous, gray-haired woman continually ran her hands through her unkempt hair. At times, she appeared to be tormented. She was continually on my mind as someone whom I did not want to "fall between the cracks."

One day after reading her social history, I decided to try a new approach to involve Mary in something she might find meaningful. She had raised a large family and had never worked outside of her home. Therefore, I decided my first attempt would be with laundry. Hopefully, this was something she would be familiar with. I didn't know how much she could comprehend so I always spoke to her as if she did comprehend. On this day, I observed her nervously standing alone with a lost look in her eyes. As she stood by a table, she appeared overwhelmed by the large room and amount of people as she stared into the large space. I approached her from the front with a smile, an arm full of clothes and an empty laundry basket. I set the basket down on the table with the pile of wrinkled clothes beside it. Apologetically, I asked Mary if she could do me a favor.

She didn't respond so I continued, "I am very sorry to ask you, but if you have the time to fold these clothes, I would GREATLY appreciate it. I am running behind in my work and just don't have the time but I understand if you don't want to. I am going to my office and will be back later." She looked into my eyes and responded verbally but I couldn't understand her words. At the time I was asking, I could not tell if she understood me. Although I was trying to keep eye contact, she was distracted by all the activity in the room so I was unsure whether she was processing my request.

As I returned to my office, I wondered if she even understood what I was saying and felt uncertain whether she would fold the laundry. After working an hour in my office, I decided to return to the dining room and see where Mary was. As I walked into the dining room, I saw Mary sitting at the table with all the laundry neatly folded and placed in the basket. As I approached, she looked up at me with a smile. I couldn't believe my eyes; she was smiling and all the laundry was neatly folded. With a smile, I told her how much she had helped me and I really appreciated her help. As I picked up the full basket, Mary stood up as if she was trying to communicate, but she stopped short so I thanked her again and asked if I could give her a hug, which she accepted. As I walked back to my office with my meticulously-folded clothes, Mary slowly sat back down, watching me as I walked away. Sitting in my office perplexed, I wondered what she was trying to tell me. What did she want to communicate? Okay, now, wait a minute! I closed my office door (in case Mary might appear) and guiltily, I threw all the neatly-folded clothes on the floor, messed them up and placed them back in the basket. As I left my office, soon I could see that Mary remained sitting alone at the table, with her usual sad, nervous expression. As

I approached her, she looked up and smiled in anticipation. I walked up with the basket as she stood and began to take the wrinkled clothes from the basket. As we removed the clothes, I repeated the previous story but she was already busy sorting and folding the clothes with no regard to my presence. The satisfaction of "making a connection" when many believe there is none, provides an overwhelming feeling of success.

Mary looked forward to folding clothes every day. In fact, she had figured out the location of my office. Unless she was ill, she would show up on a daily basis and stand at my office door until I arrived or until I noticed her presence. Although I couldn't understand her words, I knew that if I gave her the laundry basket filled with wrinkled clothes, she would smile, take the basket, fold them and return to my office with the clothes folded. Although there was some exchange of verbal communication, I was unsure of the frequency of connection or depth of understanding. I never really knew when she understood except when folding laundry. But I never gave up trying.

Mary frantically approached me one day as I was standing in the hallway. Her nonverbal communication revealed that she was upset about something. Her verbal communication was nonsensical as she flailed her hands trying to explain, trying to communicate, but I couldn't understand. Nervously, she continued to speak and appeared to be trying to lead me somewhere as she began walking away. I followed her to a table where four people were sitting and where Mary now stood, still frantic. I stood at the table looking and trying to figure out the cause of Mary's behavior. For a few minutes,

I exchanged small talk with the people sitting around the table and, remaining confused, slowly walked back down the hallway. A few minutes later, Mary arrived in the same frantic condition speaking in a rapid nonsensical manner. Again, I followed her to the same table and remained perplexed at what she was trying to communicate. Once again, I slowly walked down the hallway in the direction of my office. *What is she trying to tell me?? Why can't I figure this out?* Upon Mary's third frantic visit, I was led to a woman who was sitting in a chair in the hallway. Mary stood by her, with arms folded, as she stared at me. It was obvious the woman was very ill. As the staff and I assisted the resident, Mary calmed down and returned to the dining room where she sat down as if she had completed her mission. From that day forward, I realized I should never underestimate how much someone can understand or comprehend. Mary knew that this resident was sick and needed assistance and was persistent enough in her nonverbal communication to summon help.

On this day, the lesson for me was obvious that no one knows how, or when, this disease allows people to process information. This is an example of why people shouldn't talk in front of a person as if they are not present. You never know what, or when, someone is able to process information. It was obvious that Mary knew this resident was sick, yet she couldn't verbally tell me. But she was not going to give up until I assisted her. In all honesty, I didn't think Mary was capable of understanding if someone was sick let alone continually pursue assistance to help the person. It took me three times BUT positive communication occurred so the conclusion was worth the attempts. Patience does pay off.

My journey continued with an employment offer of a lifetime when I was hired in an executive position of an entire Alzheimer's Unit. My responsibilities ranged from admissions, selecting staff, activities, atmosphere, social services, room changes, and everything in-between. I was ecstatic to accept this position where the sociological model of healthcare was well- researched and practiced.

The Inner City

The Inner City

My first day in an executive position began in an unusual way. As I entered the building, I was informed that the Department of Health was performing an investigation. The Alzheimer's Unit was located on the third floor but there was no elevator access unless you possessed a key. The elevators were locked for safety precautions. Of course, this was for the safety of the residents who might not be aware they had entered the elevator. To many of the residents with Alzheimer's disease, the elevator looked like any other room.

As I began to climb the three flights of stairs, I heard someone screaming but couldn't understand what they were saying. As I continued to climb, the yelling became louder. Once I reached the third floor and punched in the security code, I realized the yelling was coming from my floor from a large, angry woman who was sitting in her wheelchair in the middle of the hallway. Gladys was screaming and flailing her arms, "I'm not a dog and I don't want to be treated like one. I have been able to wash myself for 96 years and I don't need anyone to help me now!" As I walked down the hallway to her she kept getting louder as she screamed at the nurse and anyone else who would listen. And she was truly on a roll. Gladys, who was a very proud person, was extremely religious. When she became upset, she sounded like an old-time preacher at a revival as her voice grew deeper and louder. And when she became upset, she had the rhythm and flavor of the old-time gospel revivals. On this day, she believed that the staff was treating her like a dog and she didn't like it. After all, she had taken care of herself for many years and couldn't understand why some stranger would tell her she needed a shower, which implied she was dirty.

Gladys was a resident who needed a lot of validation and redirection. Many times, and for many hours, she would continue to voice her opinions on the poor treatment she received from the staff. As I bent down to eye level, Gladys screamed in my face, "Do I look dirty to you?" Because I had no information about this resident, I backed up a little to avoid any possible injury just in case she became aggressive. My calm reply was, "Not at all. Did someone say you were dirty?" "Yes," she snapped, "they said I needed a shower!" At this point, I calmly tried to explain that we had reserved a shower room for her so she could take a shower. Due to the "apartment building" with so many residents, we had to schedule showers to accommodate everyone. Finally, she allowed the nurse to assist her into the shower room and make sure the water was on the proper temperature so she could clean herself. Most shower days, Gladys went through a similar routine but with much patience and perseverance, the staff could encourage her to take a shower. The whole point was to "suggest" that she might want to take a shower before the shower schedule was full. The importance of having *her make the decision* was a way to allow her to maintain her dignity and respect. Because she was the first resident I had come into contact with, I decided to read her medical chart first and see if I could find any information in her social history that would assist me in communication. Once again, obtaining a social history is extremely important when trying to understand and communicate with persons diagnosed with Alzheimer's disease. In addition, I felt that it was important to demonstrate my respect for her by calling her "Miss Gladys."

Miss Gladys' social history revealed she had never been married, had owned several homes and had taken very good care of her friends, neighbors, and family, including her nieces and nephews. Also, she had started and owned a restaurant. Upon admission, her MMSI (Mini-Mental-State-Examination) revealed 27 points of thirty, which is an excellent score.

A twist to this situation was that Miss Gladys truly believed that the restaurant she had once owned was, in fact, the facility dining room. On a daily basis, she complained about the poor quality of food because when she first started the restaurant, the portions were larger and seasoned better. She used to say, "See this crooked old little finger? The sausages aren't even this size. When I started, they were twice the size of this crooked finger. I'm not getting any nourishment. I can't live this way!" In her mind, she believed this was her restaurant and she wanted changes made to improve the quality. *After all, she was the owner.* She believed that she had started the "restaurant" in the facility and most days she continually repeated, "This food isn't fit for a dog." Because of her ongoing food complaints, it was important to monitor her weight. While monitoring her weight, we discovered that she was actually gaining weight.

I tried to validate her feelings about the quality of food, made excuses, apologies and even attempted many different scenarios but none of them ever worked. We ordered her double portions of food but this still didn't please her. We bought her seasonings but they didn't please her. The only days she was truly happy with the food was when the staff would prepare her favorite foods in the small kitchen located beside my office. On these days, you could hear her down the hallway yelling, "Praise God, Praise Jesus, this is the way the food should be. . .thank you, Jesus!" Miss Gladys had several concerns that she took very seriously. Whether her concerns were valid was irrelevant because they were valid in her mind, and I could see the distress in her face, hear it in her voice and observe it nonverbally.

Miss Gladys was extremely loud when voicing her concerns (you could hear her all the way down the hallway) and the other residents didn't, or couldn't, understand why she was yelling. Many days, other residents would become upset due to the yelling. Sometimes they thought she was yelling at them and would yell back. On these days, the staff remained busy trying to assume the monumental task of calming Miss Gladys down and also restoring a calm environment in the dining room. But for whatever reason, Miss Gladys enjoyed the attention and usually continued.

One day as I arrived at work, Miss Gladys was sitting outside my office. As I approached, she said in a stern yet sad voice, "Are you the man in charge?" I replied, "Yes" and was told in a very serious manner that she had something she needed to discuss with me. As we sat in my office discussing her real estate and family, I took extensive notes. Among the notes were addresses of her real estate and names of family members with telephone numbers. During our meeting, I realized that this woman, who appeared both physically and verbally intimidating, was hard of hearing, and very passionate about the subjects she discussed. The more passionate she became, the louder her voice would become. Simply stated, she just wanted to move back to her home where she had lived the past 60 years and couldn't understand why she was not allowed to go home. I also learned she had owned several small businesses, had opened her home to the homeless, bought many gifts for people and purchased real estate for her family members. She was a religious woman with a very strong belief in her faith.

One family member's name kept coming up in the conversation and this was the situation that brought her such sadness, distress, and confusion. As we ended our meeting, I promised Miss Gladys I would check into the situation and see if I could locate any information. Because she was so confused about owning the restaurant inside the facility, I was unsure of what I would find. I even wondered if any of the information she provided would be correct.

The only fact I was sure of was that Miss Gladys was extremely sad and angry. I knew that I must do whatever I could to put her at ease. After all, if her story was true, this wonderful woman who was 96 years old had spent most of her life giving to others and contributing so much to her family and community, I didn't want her spending her last days upset, sad and angry. And even if her story wasn't true, it was her reality and I wanted to assist her in finding peace and happiness.

As I began investigating, I realized that the addresses checked out and, much to my surprise, she was still listed in the telephone book at her previous residence. What? How can she remember these facts and still think she owns the facility kitchen and dining room? I began calling contact names that were in her medical chart and made an appointment with a relative for the next day.

Nothing could have prepared me for the meeting. I learned that a family member who had been living with Miss Gladys had stolen her life savings from the bank and, due to Miss Gladys' confusion, convinced her to sign over her home. She then placed her in the facility and sold the home. This family member's action had caused a split in the family and family members no longer communicated with each other. Due to her confusion, it became very clear to me that Miss Gladys needed a guardian, whether a family member, friend, or the state, to look after her financial and medical affairs. In addition, a state agency called Adult Protective Services was contacted to do an investigation.

And now, being burdened and saddened with this information,

I tried to devise a plan that would relieve some of her anger and sadness. I decided to meet with a family member who visited frequently. No one wanted to become a guardian for Miss Gladys. After I received the proper documentation from her physician, I filed the necessary papers with the court to request that the state grant a guardian.

When the process began, the appointed guardian visited with Miss Gladys and explained the procedure. Of course, Miss Gladys couldn't understand why she, as an adult, would need a guardian. And as always, she couldn't understand why she just couldn't go home. The process, although long and drawn out, finally concluded with a state guardian to oversee Miss Gladys' medical and financial affairs.

The staff did everything possible to ease her burdens. We would go to the local restaurants and buy her meals that she enjoyed immensely. We tried to involve her in activities, but she always declined.

The only time she would leave her room was at meal time or to use the telephone. She still remembered the telephone numbers and addresses of her relatives. Many of the numbers had been disconnected, but some were still current. When she found someone she knew, her constant discussion was on the subject of how her relative, whom she had loved and helped, put her in this situation. This situation, which she just couldn't understand, consumed her life.

Miss Gladys had lived in the facility for approximately a year. By this time, she had severe arthritis in her legs and could barely walk. Although she could transfer herself to and from the bed, she always used a wheelchair. She would usually not make it to the bathroom when needed. The staff wanted to preserve her dignity and respect, but at the same time, we wanted to assist her. Miss Gladys did not like to be "helped." After all, once again, she had always gone to the bathroom on her own. Physical therapy was asked to evaluate and treat her to see if they could help her regain any strength in her gait so she would not be a fall risk when she transferred from her bed to wheelchair. But Miss Gladys refused the therapy and any prescribed pain medications.

One day, we found out that Miss Gladys was using the trashcan for a toilet because it was next to her bed and she couldn't transfer herself from the bed to the wheelchair to the bathroom in time to avoid an "accident," which was very embarrassing for her. We placed a portable toilet beside her bed but never mentioned that we knew her secret. Several times, we attempted to explain the toilet was just in case she was in a hurry. Miss Gladys, being a strong-minded woman, refused to use the bedside commode and completely denied that she needed it. Because she was too weak and unsteady to transfer by herself, the staff feared she might fall and injure herself. We tried to explain many times that she could use her call light and we would come and assist her to the bathroom; these requests always fell on deaf ears. If we even tried to discuss the situation, Miss Gladys would fly into a rage about the fact that she was not a baby and would not be treated like one. Nothing we tried worked. Miss Gladys was not going to budge on this and we could not force her to use the call light. It is important to bring up the fact that most residents had toileting schedules to reduce "accidents." And many residents didn't know when they needed to use the bathroom until it was too late. So, every two hours, the staff would approach residents who were at risk and in a calm, polite manner would ask them if they would like to "freshen-up." Due to skin breakdown, it is very important that people are kept dry and clean. Still, Miss Gladys would decline assistance when the staff made their rounds. On a daily basis, we observed the time of day that Miss Gladys usually needed the restroom and a nurse or certified nursing assistant stood quietly outside her door waiting for her. When she was in a hurry, she easily accepted assistance.

The traumatic experience created by Miss Gladys' family was forever in her mind. She could never understand why her family member betrayed and abandoned her. We were successful for short periods of time in distracting her from her problem, but Miss Gladys, would always return to the subject that brought her great pain. She continued to believe she owned the restaurant and never liked the way it was managed.

Much to the sadness of the staff, Miss Gladys passed away a couple of days before Christmas with her family at her side. I continue to wish that the staff could have given her more peace of mind, but sometimes we are limited in what we can provide. We did provide a loving, compassionate environment and listened to all her concerns while we treated her with dignity and respect. And the many times she was happy will always remain in my heart.

Hazel, Miss Gladys' roommate, was oblivious to the fact that her roommate had passed. She didn't appear to closely observe her surroundings.

Hazel and Ruby

Hazel, a very pleasant, very confused woman, enjoyed walking up and down the hallway. She didn't initiate conversation but would gladly engage in a short one if someone initiated it. Her conversations always ended with a smile and "Well, I've gotta go." Every day, she would stroll down the hallway with her head down and arms behind her back. Once she reached one end of the hallway, forgetting her destination, she would turn around and walk in the opposite direction. Every time she passed by, I would smile, greet her with the proper greeting for the time of day and ask, "Where you goin'?" Although most Alzheimer patients in the middle-to-later stages cannot be helped by "reality orientation," I would always use the correct time so she would know, just in case she understood. Of course, many times I would receive the response, "Oh, is it morning? I thought it was evening," or vice versa. On every pass, I would say the same words except for changing the time of day.

When asked her destination, Hazel's responses were always

the same. She was either headed to the front door to look for her family, or to her room to look for her family. The front was whichever direction she was traveling and I would never try to confuse her by telling her anything different. Sometimes while eating, she would suddenly stand up and, when asked where she was going, she would say that her brother was supposed to visit so she needed to go to the front to look for him because he would not know where she was. Unfortunately, her brother had passed away many years ago. She was easily redirected by staff saying that he had car trouble or he was going to visit after her meal.

One day, on a walk down the hallway, I noticed that Hazel had placed a nightgown over her clothing. When I questioned her about the new "dress," she was completely oblivious to the situation. She had placed her nightgown over her slacks, a blouse and sweater and didn't realize she had a nightgown on over two layers of clothing. When I asked the staff about it, they said they had given her the nightgown and told her to put it on because it was getting close to bedtime. With no one telling her to remove her dirty clothing first, she did exactly as she was asked. With this level of cognitive deficit, it is extremely important to break down tasks into smaller tasks. The smaller tasks are easier to understand and comprehend. Simplification is the key, as is being very concise with instructions.

Many times, patients will literally do what is asked but due to their cognitive deficit, they will do *only* what is requested. In these instances, it is important to tell the person that they need to remove their clothes and put the clean ones on.

And because they have limited memory, staff or family must observe to see if they can follow these simple requests.

When this is not possible, it's important to assist them in removing their clothes and replacing them with clean ones. So with Hazel, someone should have waited as she took off her dirty clothes and replaced them with clean ones.

It is important that everyone with Alzheimer's disease do as much for themselves as possible so they don't forget. Therefore, if someone needs guidance but can still continue to get up and get dressed but only with assistance, it is important to gently guide them by saying for example, "would you like to wear this, or this?" Depending on cognitive deficit, a general rule is to give them no more than two choices. Many times, if someone doesn't understand how to button their sweater, the staff or family member can button their own sweater and ask the person to mirror what they did, or if they cannot brush their hair, then a staff member can brush their own hair as the person holds a brush and ask them to do the same activity. Some people pick up these tasks quickly while others cannot. It is important to never FORCE anyone to do anything they do not want to do. If you can see that the person simply cannot button their sweater or brush their hair, you should stop. If you continue to insist, you will create a problem situation. Maintaining the stage of activity is important but forcing someone to do something they can no longer remember how to do, can create sadness, confusion and anger. Observing nonverbal communication is always important.

Hazel, who had great difficulty understanding verbal

communication, would sit in the dining room and if someone was talking loudly or yelling, she always believed that they were yelling at her and would become irate. When this occurred, this sweet, timid woman would use some very off-color words. When staff would tell her that the other person was not talking about her, her anger was resolved quickly and she would continue with her previous activity. Some people become easily agitated or distracted by noise. Noise can be defined as loud music, loud talking, a television, popping gum, or the like.

One day, I heard screaming from down the hallway and ran to a location that turned out to be Hazel's room. Hazel was screaming because another resident, Ruby, had inadvertently wandered into the wrong room. Ruby was usually not a threat to anyone but was extremely confused and definitely lived in an alternate reality.

When Ruby arrived at the facility, she had previously been evicted from three others due to "behaviors." Although no information could be obtained from her admission paperwork, it was obvious that she lived in a world of her own. When she arrived, she wore a wig that was crooked most days and rarely spoke, but when she did, she spoke in a soft, mumbling, nonsensical manner. She usually would point and want you to go somewhere. Many times, she would grab your hand or arm and start leading you as she talked. It was extremely difficult to communicate with this 87-year-old woman because she lived in such a different reality. After several months of engaging Ruby in conversation on a daily basis, she began speaking often but always in her soft, mumbling, nonsensical style.

Although I never understood any of her sentences, when I asked her, "Is your name Ruby?" she could answer correctly. But, if I asked her, "What is your name?" she would not respond and would appear preoccupied.

When Miss Ruby wasn't napping, she enjoyed following the staff and residents persistently, no matter their destination. This irritated many residents but the staff would accommodate her. Many times, she would grab the staffs' hands or arms with a "grip of steel," and it was very difficult to proceed with your daily activities.

Ruby relied on the staff for all her ADL needs. ADL means Activities of Daily Living, and she was one of our most dependant ambulatory residents. She needed assistance dressing, eating, toileting and walking. Ruby was easily distracted by movement, people and noise. So if you did get her to the dining room, it was important to remain with her. It was also important to have her food ready when she sat down. If not, she would stand up and walk away and you would need to begin the process again. Many times, when short-staffed, there was a continual process of trying to get her to walk back into the dining room and sit in her chair. If the staff feeding her did not stay, she would immediately stand up and walk away. Some days when Ruby was restless, I would walk with her, hoping she would become tired enough so that when we arrived back at the dining room she would want to sit down in her chair to rest. I always spoke to her, as with all the clients, in an adult manner, explaining what we were doing and where we were going. I will never know if she understood, but I believe that she did understand some of my sentences.

Ruby would sometimes come out of her room not realizing that she didn't have her clothes on. Or, she would have only the top or bottom half of her clothing on as she walked down the hallway. The staff would rush to her and guide her back to her room and assist her with dressing. Once again, if she didn't want to go, she wouldn't. Therefore, it was essential to talk in a calm, slow tone as you tried to guide her to the appropriate destination.

As we talk about walking with a resident, now is a good time to recommend that you never pull, push, or coerce someone to walk where, or when, they don't want to. Also, never walk at a faster pace. Not only is it disrespectful but it could create aggressive behaviors. Think about someone tugging and pulling on you to try and get you to walk somewhere, and then remember that if you, with good cognitive ability, do not like it, imagine how someone with lower cognitive function would feel or react. But on another note, it is appropriate, in a calm tone and demeanor to strongly suggest that a person move in a predetermined direction.

As I reported for work one morning, I entered the hallway to find a resident whom I didn't know walking in front of me. As I came closer, I was still unsure of her identity until I arrived next to her. Ruby was walking down the hallway without her wig. I had never seen her without her wig. She had very little hair and I wondered if she had appeared in public that way before. Since she could not communicate this information, I immediately went to her room to search for the wig, which I couldn't find. After a comprehensive search of the unit, we still couldn't find it. I purchased several scarves for Ruby to wear. A few days later, the wig returned with the clean laundry. Bleach and chemicals used to wash the clothes had ruined it.

When I contacted a family member, I learned that Ruby never went anywhere without wearing one of her many wigs. The relative said that if Ruby knew she wasn't wearing her hair, she would be very embarrassed. We purchased her a new wig with the relative's assistance. Although she was not capable of understanding that she wasn't wearing her wig, it was very important to preserve her previous lifestyle, dignity and respect.

As mentioned previously, Ruby was incapable of telling us her needs. So, when a male resident was found in her room, both of them partially undressed, she could not communicate what had happened. An investigation was performed. Due to the gravity of the situation, a 24-hour watch was put on the male resident. Because of Ruby's need for attachment, it was very difficult keeping her separated from the other resident in common areas and a motion detector on a stand was placed in her room. If anyone entered the room the motion detector would sound a loud alarm.

Sometimes, it is important to check on staff in facilities, whether you are an employee or family member. I decided that I would arrive unannounced at the facility. I had already assessed Ruby and her motion detector: she was unaffected by the loud blaring siren. In fact, she had no reaction when it activated. This piercing siren could be heard all the way down the long hallway, but Ruby, with her very low cognitive level, would act as if nothing had happened. Therefore, I knew that she could not turn the system on or off because she was oblivious to the fact that it was there.

I arrived at work one Sunday to find the motion detector turned off and aimed at the wall. I turned the alarm on and waited to see if I would receive any kind of staff response. Remember, this was a situation where someone was at risk for inappropriate sexual contact with another resident. This serious situation, a State Department of Health reportable offense, was multiplied by the fact that Ruby could not defend herself, or communicate to anyone what happened. The importance of the staff protecting her was monumental.

About five minutes passed when a nurse entered the room to find me and another department head. When we asked her why the motion detector was turned off and repositioned to face the wall, she explained that Ruby had turned it off and repositioned it. "No way," I said. On Monday, the motion detector was attached to the wall above the door so there would be no confusion among the staff. The motion detector remained until we relocated the male resident to another facility, and the staff never knew when I or another department head might show up to ensure the procedure was not jeopardized. When a loved one or family member is institutionalized, it is appropriate to visit at different days and times to check on the quality of care. Is there an appropriate amount of staff? Do they receive the same quality of care during all shifts? Does the staff treat all residents in a calm manner? Are they compassionate? Do they show empathy? These are important facts to remember when you are researching healthcare facilities.

Don and Alonzo

The male resident I mentioned previously was named Don. He had a mental illness combined with dementia. Because there are few behavior units with mental facilities, it was a difficult task to have him moved. In addition, most facilities would not want to accept the liability of having a resident who had been found with a female resident in a compromising position. Don, a tall man who rarely spoke unless spoken too, usually carried a Bible. He enjoyed therapeutic chores and swept the dining area after every meal. He was nonsocial but when he talked, it was about the Bible.

As I was observing him one day, I noticed that he was walking alone down the hallway, with his hand to his ear having a conversation. He walked into his room and left a few minutes later with clothes on hangers in his arms. I left my office and walked up to him as he continued walking and said, "Hey Don, what you doing?" Without missing a step, Don told me he was going home and that his preacher was on his way to give him a ride. When I asked, "When did you speak to your preacher?" he replied that he had just gotten off the telephone with him. He then placed a chair by an exit door and returned to his room for more clothes.

Because Don had a mental illness and was having auditory hallucinations, I didn't know if validation therapy would help or hurt the situation. I walked up to Don when he was in his room getting more clothes, and said that I had talked to the preacher: he was having car trouble and would not be able to give Don a ride. As we talked, the staff moved his clothes to a secure location.

Don said, "Well, what is his name because I just talked to him." I replied, "He didn't give me his name, he just told me that he was your preacher and to please tell you that he was having car trouble and would not be able to give you a ride today." Don reluctantly returned to his room.

The next day, Don resumed this behavior but it began early in the morning. With his hand to his ear, Don was having a conversation while walking alone down the hallway. He placed a chair by the door and started piling his clothes on it. After several trips from his room with his and his roommate's clothing, the clothes began piling up. Don was unaware that the staff was removing his clothing from the chair every time he returned to his room for more. We always left a few items of clothing, and Don was never the wiser.

Finally, I approached Don and tried the same therapeutic fib as the previous day. He did not believe me this time. He insisted that the preacher was on his way and he didn't want to miss his ride. Don remained by the door for the entire day. Because of his mental illness, auditory hallucinations and behavior, I decided that he needed to be sent for an evaluation at a psychiatric hospital.

I called every psychiatric hospital that I could think of but was told repeatedly that his acuity rate was not high enough to warrant a transfer. They based his evaluation solely on his acuity rate (the rate of severity), believing that he was not a danger to himself or others. I explained to the psychiatric staff that he could not be re-directed and he was having auditory hallucinations and had been found partially clothed in a female's room. They all said that his acuity rate was not high enough and to call again if something else happened that would change his rating.

One Saturday afternoon, I received a telephone call at home: Don had jumped out of a third floor window. Although the staff had seen him at the window earlier, they didn't think he would jump. You can never underestimate the willpower of someone who has Alzheimer's disease or mental illness. Don had made up his mind he was going to leave, and the unlocked window gave him the opportunity.

The good news was that Don was okay. He had landed on a canopy that broke his fall. He then rolled over, fell into the shrubbery, brushed himself off, picked up his Bible and said he was going to see his wife. We sent Don to the emergency room for an evaluation. Because there was no physical harm, he was released, much to the dismay of the facility administrator, who was trying to keep him in the hospital until I could find him a new home.

On Sunday, I returned to work to call the psychiatric hospitals to see if his acuity rate was high enough for admission to their facilities. I was shocked to hear that his acuity rate was too high for the first hospital and they wouldn't take him. Thankfully, the second hospital accepted him for observation.

On Monday, after several telephone discussions, I met with a social worker to discuss having Don admitted to her facility, which admitted people with problem behaviors. Although I was honest, I didn't immediately reveal that Don had recently jumped out the window. Finally, I discussed all the details with her and explained that I did not want him "labeled" as someone with disruptive or dangerous behaviors because the stigma would follow him for the rest of his life.

Don had always been very polite and helpful. There was no evidence that anything had happened in the female resident's room and if the psychiatric hospitals would have accepted him for an evaluation, I believe the situation would have been avoided. He had never shown signs of problems or behaviors, and medical tests had all come back okay. So it was important that he not be classified as someone with behaviors. When someone is classified with problem behaviors, a whole new world of problems can open up for them, including strong medications to control their behaviors. I didn't want this to happen to Don.

Although Don had been moving his roommate's and his clothing in the previous weeks, the time had come for him to finally move to his new home. I arranged to have all his belongings transferred, and I personally set up his room close to the way it was previously arranged. Don made a smooth move and fit easily into his new environment. His old roommate, Alonzo, was oblivious to the fact that furniture was moved out, and was not even aware that his roommate had moved.

Alonzo had moderate cognitive impairment, and a problem with his short-term memory. In fact, after he finished his meals, he would inevitably go to his room to use the bathroom and return five minutes later and ask, "Is it time to eat?" Alonzo was fun-loving and always smiling and telling jokes until he felt someone was in trouble; then he would want to go to their defense.

Apparently, he had been a boxer and enjoyed telling other residents about his boxing experiences. Unfortunately, some of the residents would misunderstand when Alonzo said, "I used to fight." They heard only the word "fight" and thought he was asking them to fight. Therefore it was important to observe him and listen to what he was saying, because his anger could explode in a second. Every day, Alonzo offered one or more residents a ride in his van that he believed was parked in the parking lot. He would often ask me if I could show him how to get to the parking lot.

I would explain to Alonzo that his van was being worked on and I was waiting for the mechanic to call me when it was finished. Sometimes he would ask what was wrong with the van, and other days he would just say, "Well, come and get me when they call." Alonzo was always easily redirected when discussing his van and continued to offer rides to many of the residents.

He had a heart of gold and had lived in the same room for five years. Because he enjoyed socializing, his room was by the main dining room and activity area. Due to his extreme confusion and short-term memory deficit, I felt it was important that he never be moved to a different room. He had great difficulty processing information and I knew a move would totally disrupt his life. This belief was made known to the administrator.

One day my administrator came to me and said he wanted to give Alonzo's room to a new resident. To make matters worse, he wanted us to move Alonzo immediately. As the administrator stood over the charge nurse and myself, waiting for us to make the telephone call to the responsible family member, both of us were shocked and in disbelief that he would order this change; we knew what the future would bring. The nurse made the call to the family member and instead of requesting permission, the administrator ordered us to tell the responsible party that we had to move Alonzo. Despite protest and confusion by the family member, we moved Alonzo.

In the state where I work, it is illegal (and unethical) to move residents from room to room without justification. Once a "patient" is moved into a long-term healthcare facility they become a "resident." The institution becomes the residence, therefore, there are specific rights implemented by the law to ensure adequate care is given and no civil or federal laws are broken. In all states, there are "Residents' Rights." Please check with your local State Department of Health to obtain a copy. In my state, there must be a medical or psychosocial need, and permission must be granted in advance by a person responsible for the resident's care, such as a family member with power of attorney, or guardian.

The administrator had ordered us to move him four doors away from where he currently lived. I placed a big sign with his name on the door and the nurse and I placed all his belongings in the same location as his previous room, hanging pictures and placing knick-knacks in the hope that he would feel at home. But this plan was unsuccessful.

From the very beginning, the room change was a nightmare not only for Alonzo, but also for the staff. For two weeks he continued to go into his old room and was redirected by staff many times on a daily basis. He was so confused. Some days, he would ask for a ride to his home, and other days he believed that he was on the wrong floor of his previous apartment building and asked us how to get to the 12th floor. Sometimes, he would become agitated when the staff redirected him to his new room, and other times he just appeared confused. After all, he had lived in his old room for five years, which was an eternity for Alonzo.

As the weeks turned into a month, Alonzo was not getting any better. We had a psychiatric evaluation performed and his medications were increased, to no avail. He was becoming more and more confused about everything and now, easily agitated.

And his nonverbal communication revealed depression. He had attended many activities in the past, but after his room change, he would remain inside until meal times and refused many activities as he was no longer interested.

One day after his old room became vacant and the administrator was not present, the nurse and I worked at record speed to call his responsible party and move Alonzo back to his original room. After several days, he was back to his regular self.

To this happy-go-lucky resident, something as small as a room change was detrimental. He was affected in a very strong, negative manner. In addition, the staff working with him were also affected by the negative change in his personality. Although he was back to his regular self, the experience confirms that someone as confused as Alonzo should never be moved except in rare cases when special circumstances require it.

Phyllis and Mildred

Phyllis and Mildred seemed like perfect roommates. Mildred, who had moved in recently, retained her large suitcase that she packed daily. The problem was that she would also pack her roommate's clothes and anything else that would fit inside.

Phyllis, who needed assistance with dressing and toileting, never realized that her clothes were missing. The staff who assisted her in dressing each morning would not be able to find her clothes. But, her clothes were easily located in Mildred's closet. And Mildred was very possessive of all her belongings, including her purse, suitcase, and everything else within sight.

One day, during meal time, with the family's permission, I went into their room, unpacked the suitcase and removed it. The suitcase was never mentioned, or remembered by Mildred but she continued to fold and stack her and anyone else's clothing on her bed.

In addition, Mildred hoarded so many items that her room had to be checked on a daily basis for safety and health reasons. When she walked down the hallway, you could plainly see that her purse was so full that it wouldn't close. And, her purse was always kept within sight. She also collected items in her pockets and sometimes inside her sweatshirt or jacket. Although it was obvious that items were bulging from her clothing, the staff always pretended not to see. When Mildred finally cleaned out her purse and stored the items in the drawers, the staff would remove them. If another resident was missing something, we would begin our search in her room, and usually found the missing item. If not, we would move on to the next person who could have possibly taken the item, oblivious to the fact that it wasn't theirs.

It was extremely important to do this when no one was in the room. If either resident saw you with something they thought was theirs, it was imperative that you return it with a calm explanation, or inevitably an argument would ensue. The purpose of the daily checks was to return the items to the rightful owner, or dispose of hoarded food or milk that had spoiled.

The secret daily checks were performed in such a way that conflict was usually avoided, due to the fact that both residents did not remember what they had hoarded or improperly taken. But, if I was caught in the act of removing the items, I would get the same story: "That's mine and you can't have it." Whenever this occurred, I simply apologized and gave the item back. I always knew that either a staff member or I could retrieve it later. The main concern was preserving dignity and respect, and avoiding confrontation. Hoarding is often found in healthcare facilities: silverware, cartons of milk, napkins, salt, sugar, bread. I have seen many staff members deal with hoarding in different ways. From the very beginning, I learned that reasoning and logic did not work, and I could try for hours, but the residents would only become aggressive. Unless hoarding is a true problem, such as with milk or food, I would always downplay the problem and remove items when they were not in their room. I would never confront them about the situation, as this would have been futile.

Both residents were very paranoid, to say the least. I remember the day I tried to give Phyllis the MMSE. I always try to put a resident at ease before the MMSE by sitting and talking with them before I ask any questions. When I began asking this resident questions, she became very defensive, "My husband answers all my questions for me," she barked in a loud tone. I said, "Well, I just spoke with him and he said that this time it was okay to answer the questions." So she began the MMSE.

After the first question, I could see that she felt uncomfortable and didn't really know the answers to questions such as: What year is it? What is the date? What county are we in? What state are we in? Where are you now? etc. Experience had taught me that I needed to be very tender and understanding while giving this exam. I didn't want to embarrass the resident, or make her feel uncomfortable, so I decided to stop the questioning, and we sat and discussed enjoyable topics for awhile. When I finished, I thanked her for talking with me and departed.

Both of these strong-minded, paranoid women didn't like to take showers. In fact, they hated showers. I have learned many reasons why, but as always, never all the reasons. Some people were modest and embarrassed to undress in front of someone. Some didn't shower often. Some were afraid of the water. Some believed they were being touched inappropriately. Some were afraid of the sterile-looking shower room. The list goes on and on. To avoid confrontation, I do not believe in forcing someone to take a shower.

Depending on who we were communicating with, we would try different tactics when trying to get someone to shower. Many times, the person had been incontinent and was totally unaware that they had a horrible odor. In this instance, due to possible skin breakdown because of the unsanitary condition, we would try to persuade a resident to shower, or at least clean up a little. Of course, you should never go up to the person and state, "You have had a bowel movement and need to be cleaned." To preserve dignity and respect, the staff used different approaches.

There is never one specific approach to take when trying to direct, or redirect someone, but using patience, persistence and a calm approach will work sooner or later. Sometimes it takes longer than others. Usually, approaching a resident in a calm manner and a different approach 15-20 minutes later will yield positive results. Many times having another person approach also yields positive results.

I have used many approaches from, "Your husband, (or friend, or relative) is coming to visit; would you like to freshen up?" Or sometimes, "The laundry just returned these clothes; would you like to put them on after you freshen up?" Whatever works for you. . .use it!

Judy and a Paranoid World

One of my most challenging yet rewarding residents was named Judy. She was a very sweet, soft-spoken, scared, paranoid woman. But when she smiled her beautiful big brown eyes lit up the room. On the day she arrived from the hospital, Judy's eyes revealed fear and confusion. I escorted her to her room and we sat and talked.

This very confused, pleasant woman didn't understand why she was here and wanted to go home. I assured her that she was here to get better because she had been in the hospital and needed to recover. She asked many questions, stating that she didn't have any money for room or board. I told her that her room and board had been taken care of. I gave her a tour of the locked unit and made sure she arrived in the dining room at meal time.

Judy appeared very frail. I escorted her to her table and brought her the meal. Much to my surprise, she ate everything and wanted more. I brought her another plate and she finished it. I was surprised that such a small, frail woman could eat so much. It looked like she had not eaten in days as she hurriedly ate her food. Every meal she thoroughly enjoyed and her appetite amazed me. And like clock-work, she would come to me after every meal and whisper in my ear that the woman across from her was stealing the silverware, but warned me not to look at her because she would know Judy was talking about her. Of course, we were well aware that this was a resident who was a hoarder.

I was curious if I could locate any family or friends so that I could obtain information about this very colorful woman. She wore her wig daily and many days with a colorful scarf, or whatever she could find to wrap around her head. The only information that I could obtain was from her admission paperwork sent from the hospital. She was single, lived alone, with a diagnosis of Alzheimer's disease with paranoia. Her admission paperwork revealed that she had been found by the police wandering on a busy highway, lost, confused, and looking for her home. No one knew how she arrived at the highway since she didn't own a car couldn't drive and she herself couldn't explain. Nevertheless, she was taken to the hospital for evaluation. The hospital evaluation revealed that her cognition was impaired and she could not properly take care of herself. Therefore, after her hospital stay she moved into our facility on the locked unit to prevent her from wandering away.

This small, frail woman displayed her emotions, whether sad, happy, or frightened, through her beautiful brown eyes, and when it came time for me to leave for the day, she asked me, "But what will I do?" as her eyes displayed fright and sadness.

I explained to her that I was going home but would return in the morning. Although she was frightened and didn't want me to leave, I repeatedly assured her that many of my friends (employees) were there to "keep her safe." All day, I shared her information with staff members and introduced them to her one by one. As I left her room she requested that I close the door because "you know how people are, they come in and steal things." With a smile, hug and one final assurance that she would be safe, I gently closed her door.

The next morning I was greeted eagerly by the staff, who could not enter Judy's room. She had barricaded herself and wouldn't let anyone in. This was a new experience for me, to say the least. I gently knocked on her door and told her my name but, she yelled, "Go away!" After about five minutes of speaking through the partially-blocked door and explaining that it was breakfast time, she finally allowed me to enter her dark room. First, she explained she had to move some items away from the door so I could enter. I heard furniture moving but she did not leave much area to enter, so I squeezed in between the stacked items. I was shocked to see a chest of drawers, night stand, and two chairs next to the door, and still partially blocking the entrance. The curtains were pulled tightly closed with a blanket thrown over them. She said that she was afraid because someone had entered her room in the middle of the night, so she moved the furniture to block the door. (By the way, the night-time visitor was a staff member doing rounds). As we talked calmly, I slowly moved the furniture blocking the door against her strong protests, and was amazed that such a frail woman could have moved the heavy chest of drawers.

As I assisted her in getting ready for breakfast, I explained that I was concerned that if something bad happened, she would not be able to exit her room in a timely manner and the staff wouldn't be able to enter. She was not convinced. I reassured her repeatedly of her safety, but I could still see fear in her eyes. She continued barricading her room for the next week. No matter how many times or different approaches I attempted, I was not able to persuade her that she was safe. So I finally devised a plan.

Each day while she was eating breakfast, I would remove one item from her room and see if she noticed. Because she lived alone in a double room, there was twice the furniture for her to move. Still, it was important to be discreet as she was already scared and paranoid. I had a back-up plan if my mission was not successful. If she noticed anything missing, I would tell her that I sent it to be repaired or cleaned, and then a few hours later, I would return the item. I removed a chair the first day. She didn't notice, and I felt relief and optimism. The next day I removed a night stand, and still received no response about anything missing. "Great. This plan is working," I thought, so I proceeded, removing one piece of furniture everyday: a chair, a bedside table, and the chest of drawers. We also locked her bed into place so she wouldn't be able to move it.

I was so happy that there had been no confrontation, and considered this plan a great success. Well, it was a success until one morning when Judy returned to her room. She said her chest of drawers had been "stolen." I explained that it was broken and had been sent to the carpenter for repair. This did not go over well with her as she liked to remain in her room, except for meals at which time the staff had to strongly encourage her to go to the dining room. As soon as her meal was over, she would return to her room, barricade the door and watch her favorite TV programs that I would locate for her. She hadn't realized that the items she used to barricade the door were slowly missing until I had removed the chest of drawers, the last piece of furniture.

Upon arriving to her room only to find the chest missing, she immediately returned to me looking for someone to "file a complaint with." Lucky day; I was the man! I calmly explained that we had sent the chest to be repaired and cleaned. "But, I didn't want my furniture cleaned, are you saying I am dirty? I keep my home very clean." "I would never think your home is dirty, but I just wanted to surprise you and one of the drawers was broken," I replied. Over the next several days, she inquired about her furniture and I would tell her that I'd call and see when the chest would be returned. Luckily, she eventually forgot about the furniture.

I stopped by Judy's room every morning, to encourage her to come to the dining room to eat breakfast. She had convinced the staff that she couldn't leave her room for various reasons; sometimes she was ill, sometimes her "legs didn't work." I was becoming concerned that if we allowed her to stay in her room 24 hours a day, she would never leave her room. Although I never force anyone to do anything against their will, I do calmly—yet strongly—encourage certain activities. In this case, my concern for her psychosocial well-being overrode the amount of time I needed to encourage this scared, paranoid woman to exit her room every day. Upon leaving her room, she would usually decide to visit with the other residents for a while before returning to watch her favorite TV shows. And it was obvious she was enjoying herself outside of her room.

But she could always convince new staff members that her legs didn't work or she was not feeling well. It was important that I arrived in the morning before her tray was ready to be served. When providing care for people, whether in their home, or in a long-term healthcare facility, the importance of "being on the same page" is monumental. Therefore, it is important that everyone involved share information and know the particulars of the situation so that they can establish and maintain a therapeutic routine.

About two weeks into the process of helping Judy feel safe and secure in her new home, the staff witnessed a positive behavioral change. She was happy and becoming content as she continued to enjoy the wonderful food. In addition, encouraging her to leave her room became an easier task. One morning I arrived to find the administrator on my unit. He informed me that I must move Judy to a new room. After a very long, intense discussion with him, I lost the battle for her to remain and was told to move her that day. It was extremely important that I use an approach that would be acceptable to this already highly-suspicious woman who was just beginning to enjoy life.

As the nurse and I arrived at Judy's room, she was lying in bed watching her favorite television show, with her curtains pulled tightly closed and a blanket thrown over them. Her curtains were closed every time I entered the room. Although she was on the third floor, her reasoning was that she didn't want anyone looking in her window. After exchanging pleasant morning greetings, we asked Judy if we could sit down and discuss some exciting news with her. With a big smile and happiness in her eyes like a child at Christmas, she said, "Sure!"

Although the nurse and I were unhappy about the move, both of us sat down and tried to appear upbeat. I told Judy that we had a surprise for her and we had decided to move her into a nicer room with a beautiful view, a room we had remodeled just for her. I had hung pictures on the wall, placed some flowers in the room, and moved all the furniture in the same position as her current room.

This news broke her heart and turned her previously beautiful, happy brown eyes to sadness and fright. "But I don't want to move, and I have all my furniture arranged just the way I like it," she said. It was obvious from her nonverbal and verbal communication that she was frightened to move. Because the nurse and I were still in disbelief about the ordered move, we were not going to make Judy feel like she had been forced to move from what she now called her "home." We needed time to discuss and encourage her. In this instance, the administrator was breaking the law but was driven more by money than by the problems of this poor, frightened woman.

The administrator, who was becoming impatient, had retuned twice to see if the room change had taken place. He explained she had to be moved immediately due to a new arrival's need for the room. We explained the situation he was causing without success.

As the nurse and I continued talking to Judy, she became more and more upset. "I just finished painting this room," she stated sadly. I explained that the other room was beautiful and that the nurse and I had just finished painting it a special color for her. I asked her if she would go down and just look at the room and the paint color we had chosen. We successfully encouraged her to look at the room that we had prepared for her as a surprise. "A bigger room with a better view." As we left her room, I said that due to my color blindness, I couldn't tell what color she had painted her room. "White. I think it looks so clean and I used 15 cans of spray," she replied. With reluctance and sadness, we walked slowly to the new room, obeying the administrator's orders to make the move during breakfast time.

As she looked around the new room with sad eyes, she said, "I want to stay in my old room." I assured her that if she moved and was unhappy with the room for any reason, we would move her back to her old room. I was not sure I'd be able to keep this promise. We talked for a long time as I showed her all the new wall hangings, curtains and the new wall color. She said she really liked the new paint color that we had picked for her, not realizing, it was the exact same color as her other room. With sadness and fear in her eyes, and much reassurance from me, she reluctantly agreed, but upon the condition that if she didn't like it, she could return to her previous room. As always, she told me that she did not want to share her room with anyone. Since her day of admission, Judy was concerned that she would have to share her room. There were two beds in each room and she was continually concerned because she did not want anyone else living in her home.

Without the exceptionally compassionate staff, the room change could have been a disaster. Judy complained that her stomach hurt and she wasn't hungry. I could see that this move was taking a toll on her, but that we had been successful in creating a secure environment where she would be happy. Her sadness returned as she insisted that she participate in the move to ensure we moved everything, even though when she moved into the facility, she arrived with nothing and was wearing only a hospital gown.

Once the move was completed, Judy became more paranoid, believing that someone was going to come into her room even though she was directly across from the nurse's station. She remained in her room for three days where we took her meals and visited with her. She no longer cared if she wore her wig and didn't really care about watching her television anymore, which had been a daily activity that she thoroughly enjoyed.

The staff, who was sympathetic to her situation, tried to be very supportive and gave her as much attention as she needed. I learned that Judy loved cookies and chocolate. From that day forward, I always kept a special supply of goodies for her. That was one ploy that would always make her smile:

a cookie, or chocolate. Even if the smile lasted only for a couple of minutes, it was well worth seeing her eyes light up. Unfortunately, we were not successful at any intervention we tried, and due to her deteriorating condition we decided to have a physical and psychiatric evaluation performed.

After her evaluation, she was immediately placed on very strong antipsychotic medications to control her paranoia, and antidepressants for her depression. The medications made her very lethargic and she lost her appetite, falling asleep in the dining room at meal times. She had no quality of life and appeared to be zombie-like. We requested a medication reduction. Within a few days, she became closer to the once-happy Judy. As she began to come out of her room more and more, she became more of the person we previously knew. Still, whenever she left her room she would place a Kleenex in the door frame as she shut her door to ensure that no one else entered not realizing that it could be easily removed when entering and replaced when exiting.

During her physical evaluation, it was discovered that she had arthritis in her knees, so therapy was started. Because the physical therapy department was on another floor, the therapist decided it would be easier and less time-consuming to take her in a wheelchair to therapy than have her walk the distance.

One day at lunch time, I noticed that she was sitting in another resident's wheelchair. The residents who could walk would leave their wheelchairs in the hallway and the staff would assist them to their tables. When asked why she was sitting there, she simply stated, "They told me I couldn't walk. . .my legs don't work." When explained that she was sitting in someone else's wheelchair, she told me that she couldn't find hers. I tried to explain that the therapist transported her in a wheelchair to therapy just because of the distance; she told me, "No, they said I need a wheelchair. My legs don't work anymore."

From that day forward, we tried to keep wheelchairs away from her because of the fear that one day she would truly believe that she couldn't walk, and stop walking completely. If she believed this was *her reality* then she would convince herself and not walk. In fact, whenever she saw a staff member, she would walk slowly and stumble like she was going to fall. As they should, healthcare professionals took her complaint seriously. The problem was that when she didn't think the staff was watching, she walked perfectly. She didn't realize that we had cameras and monitors throughout the unit and had observed her many times walking normally. But, as soon as she saw one of us, she would grab for the railing, as if she were falling. As I was visiting with Judy one day, much to my surprise, a visitor showed up looking for her.

Finally, I would be able to inquire about her past and, I hoped, gain some insight into her reality that led to her peculiar behaviors. I introduced myself to her guest and asked if we could meet after her visit. She happily agreed to come to my office later.

Judy's friend took the time to answer my many questions concerning Judy's social history. For the first time, I understood the many aspects of this beautiful, frail woman's life. I better understood *her reality* and why she did so many activities that appeared odd or dysfunctional to me. Judy's visitor was an ex-neighbor who looked after her, purchased her groceries and assisted in paying bills.

According to the neighbor, Judy was a quiet, nonsocial person who never left her home. She had moved about 40 years ago from Chicago. She was never married and had always lived alone in her home. The neighbor couldn't remember a time when Judy had a visitor. The only family member the ex-neighbor was aware of was an older sister in Chicago who was in poor health. Judy had nailed boards up on the downstairs windows because her home had been burglarized three times within the last two years.

The neighbor said Judy enjoyed sitting by the front door with the door slightly cracked open so she could see out. One day, a man who had burglarized a neighbor's home was running from the police while they searched the area. Because her door was partially open, the man ran into Judy's home and encountered her. He remained with her for several hours as the police searched the neighborhood, but did not harm her. Becoming inpatient, the burglar donned one of Judy's wigs and some clothes, and departed. The police apprehended him a short time later.

Judy's only comment concerning the ordeal was that he had smoked too many of her cigarettes. So many of her behaviors that appeared odd now made sense. An elderly person living alone with no friends might become depressed and paranoid, especially after experiencing multiple burglaries.

After speaking to her ex-neighbor, I realized that her "behaviors" made sense. Her curtains were always closed because her windows at home had been boarded up. Thank goodness we didn't have any boards lying around because she was very engineering and would have found a way to board up her windows.

She was nonsocial in the facility due to the fact that her personality in general was nonsocial. She had few visitors, and the ones she had were uninvited. She was concerned about people entering her room due to the many burglaries in her past. Many of her behaviors made sense now, although her paranoia was extreme and did require medicine to control.

If the first move wasn't bad enough, the administrator returned one day with the same request: he needed her room for another new admission. Totally discouraged, I explained the problems the staff had experienced during the last move, and most importantly, how the move had affected the resident. His response was, "Make the move happen." Because of her past history, paranoia and nonsocial behavior, I argued that the move would never work and would only harm Judy, who was still accepting her first move. I received the same response: "Make it happen."

This move not only saddened Judy, but also angered the staff. The nurse and I went into Judy's room to tell her the bad news. Of course, we tried once again to appear upbeat. Our approach didn't work any better than it did the first time.

Judy became very distraught as she assisted us in moving all her belongings to the new room. I asked her what her favorite color was and printed a huge sign with her name written in royal blue and placed it on her new door. I hung her pictures and bought her some new knick-knacks to take her mind off the move.

Judy believed that she was being evicted for not paying her rent. I typed up a large sign that read: "Judy has paid her rent until the end of the year," signed it and placed it on her wall. She returned to her old room daily and would lie down on the bed if the resident wasn't there. Once she was lying down, it became very difficult to encourage her to get up. She would not accept the fact that it was someone else's room.

I worked late several nights so I could try and help Judy understand that she lived in a new "home." It was heartbreaking to observe her slightly open her door, look in both directions, then slowly walk down the hallway to her old room. She would look around to see if any one was watching and then slowly open the door and walk in. We tried to deter her entrance by placing a large medicine cart in front of her old door, but Judy—confused, sad and frail—would still be able to push the heavy cart away from the door. Time after time, I greeted her with a smile and calm voice before she walked into her old room. She was always concerned that she had left something in the room, so we would walk through and look in the closets, drawers, and under the bed.

Once inside, she wouldn't want to leave and would want to check everything again, just one more time. Unfortunately, she would do this as many times as we would let her. There was no way that I could rush her because of her sad, concerned demeanor. Some of her sadness about being evicted had resurfaced and she truly believed we were getting ready to put her out on the street.

Whenever she would begin talking about her eviction, I would smile and say, "But Miss Judy, don't you remember? I took care of that." Then I would go to the posted sign and read it for her. My explanation resolved the situation every time.

But she lost her appetite again. When I asked her what was wrong, she would say, "Oh, I am just worried, but don't you bother with my problems." I spent countless hours with Judy and finally she accepted her new home and returned to her previous, happy-go-lucky self. During her times of sadness, some candy or a cookie would always bring a smile to her face.

But eventually, Judy was watching her favorite television shows again in her room and enjoying life to the fullest.

Conclusion

This short, easy-to-read book is about my personal journey and the many challenges I faced and successfully resolved by using two simple techniques: validation and therapeutic fibbing. Usually, when using these techniques, results were seen immediately unless there were underlying problems.

With the ever-increasing number of people being diagnosed with Alzheimer's disease, learning how to communicate with them is essential to improving the persons' quality of life and understanding their behaviors. At this stage, life is no longer lived in reality, but in an altered state from the past. Understanding and accepting the residents' altered state, allows them to live in a reality they are comfortable with and understand. In addition, it provides security, a sense of well-being, and protects their dignity and respect when they are no longer able.

Trying to force this group of people into reality inevitably turns into disaster. As much as they try, they can't remember a familiar name, or family member, or much of anything outside of their reality. Some of my saddest times were spent listening to family members trying to convince a loved one that they knew them. It was very difficult to hear people talk about their loved ones, in front of them, as if they weren't there. Remember, no one really knows how, or when someone at this level comprehends, or how much they can comprehend. Therefore, you should never talk about the person in front of them. I remember a sister who visited frequently but was always trying to force the resident to "act right," and would say things such as, "Stop mumbling. I know you can talk better than that. Stop it! You know my name, now, what is it?"

I suggest that when greeting a loved one say, "Hi, this is your son, John. How are you today?" This way you can gauge where the person is. If the person says, "Well, I know you're my son John!" Great, then you know the person knows you. But, if they show no recognition, drop it. I have witnessed much confusion and sadness while loved ones tried to explain, at great length, that the person has to know them.

The emotional toll can be devastating for caregivers who wonder if there is any way they can communicate or if it is futile. Therefore, the importance of knowing their reality is the key to unlocking meaningful communication. In addition, it provides the caregiver a sense that someone is there, even though they communicate in a different manner.

I have had many discussions with residents' family and friends who were confused about whether their loved one knew who they were. Through my journey of observing nonverbal behavior among this select group of people, there is no doubt in my mind that most residents did know who the person was, or at least knew their visitor was someone significant in their life. Sometimes it is not clear how the connection is made, whether through tone of voice, a familiar face, or comforting touch. Many residents exhibit nonverbal and sometimes nonsensical verbal behavior that demonstrates they have been touched by their visitor in a positive way: whether a smile, increased physical activity, verbalization, or other positive communication.

My mission is to spread the word on how easy it is to communicate in a positive manner. When these techniques are performed effectively, they assist you in understanding their form of communication.

Not only will this preserve the dignity and respect of the person, but also bring you joy, due to the fact that you are communicating just on a different level. So, if you ever feel challenged, or confused by a loved one with Alzheimer's disease, I recommend that you take the time to walk in their shoes.

Acknowledgments:

Most importantly, To God
"Acknowledge Him in all ways and He will direct your path."

Katherine Martinez
Who unselfishly donated her talent and time to edit my book.

To My Clients
Who inspired me daily and influenced me
to put my experiences into words.

My life-long friends
Chris Crewell, Judy Perantoni, Marilyn Dayton,
for their continued inspiration, support, and
genuine encouragement while always
keeping it "honest and real."

Sharon Sullivan
An excellent nurse, role model, and human-being

Melinda Davis Secord
"Photography By Melinda"

For speaking engagements, or to contact Michael:
walkingintheirshoes@gmail.com

Made in the USA
Lexington, KY
13 April 2014